A Visitation
of the Plague

DANIEL DEFOE

A VISITATION
OF THE PLAGUE

PENGUIN BOOKS

PENGUIN BOOKS

Published by the Penguin Group

Penguin Books USA Inc., 375 Hudson Street,
New York, New York 10014, U.S.A.
Penguin Books Ltd, 27 Wrights Lane,
London W8 5TZ, England
Penguin Books Australia Ltd, Ringwood,
Victoria, Australia
Penguin Books Canada Ltd, 10 Alcorn Avenue,
Toronto, Ontario, Canada M4V 3B2
Penguin Books (N.Z.) Ltd, 182–190 Wairau Road,
Auckland 10, New Zealand

Penguin Books Ltd, Registered Offices:
Harmondsworth, Middlesex, England

Published in Penguin Books 1995

This extract is from *A Journal of the Plague Year* by Daniel
Defoe, edited by Anthony Burgess and Christopher Bristow,
published by Penguin Books.

ISBN 0 14 60.0159 1

Printed in the United States of America

A Visitation
of the Plague

I lived without Aldgate, about midway between Aldgate Church and Whitechappel Bars, on the left hand or north side of the street; and as the distemper had not reached to that side of the city, our neighbourhood continued very easy. But at the other end of the town their consternation was very great: and the richer sort of people, especially the nobility and gentry from the west part of the city, thronged out of town with their families and servants in an unusual manner; and this was more particularly seen in Whitechapel; that is to say, the Broad Street where I lived; indeed, nothing was to be seen but waggons and carts, with goods, women, servants, children, &c.; coaches filled with people of the better sort, and horsemen attending them, and all hurrying away; then empty waggons and carts appeared, and spare horses with servants, who, it was apparent, were returning or sent from the countries to fetch more people; besides innumerable numbers of men on horseback, some alone, others with servants, and, generally speaking, all loaded with baggage and fitted out for travelling, as anyone might perceive by their appearance.

This was a very terrible and melancholy thing to see, and as it was a sight which I could not but look on from morning to night (for indeed there was nothing else of moment to be seen), it filled me with very serious thoughts of the misery that was coming upon the city, and the unhappy condition of those that would be left in it.

This hurry of the people was such for some weeks that there was no getting at the Lord Mayor's door without exceeding difficulty; there were such pressing and crowding there to get passes and certificates of health for such as travelled abroad, for without these there was no being admitted to pass through the towns upon the road, or to lodge in any inn. Now, as there had none died in the city for all this time, my Lord Mayor gave certificates of health without any difficulty to all those who lived in the ninety-seven parishes, and to those within the liberties too for a while.

This hurry, I say, continued some weeks, that is

to say, all the month of May and June, and the more because it was rumoured that an order of the Government was to be issued out to place turnpikes and barriers on the road to prevent people travelling, and that the towns on the road would not suffer people from London to pass for fear of bringing the infection along with them, though neither of these rumours had any foundation but in the imagination, especially at first.

I now began to consider seriously with myself concerning my own case, and how I should dispose of myself; that is to say, whether I should resolve to stay in London or shut up my house and flee, as many of my neighbours did. I have set this particular down so fully, because I know not but it may be of moment to those who come after me, if they come to be brought to the same distress, and to the same manner of making their choice; and therefore I desire this account may pass with them rather for a direction to themselves to act by than a history of my actings, seeing it may not be of one farthing value to them to note what became of me.

I had two important things before me: the one was the carrying on my business and shop, which was considerable, and in which was embarked all my effects in the world; and the other was the preservation of my life in so dismal a calamity as I saw apparently was coming upon the whole city, and which, however great it was, my fears perhaps, as well as other people's, represented to be much greater than it could be.

The first consideration was of great moment to me; my trade was a saddler, and as my dealings were chiefly not by a shop or chance trade, but among the merchants trading to the English colonies in America, so my effects lay very much in the hands of such. I was a single man, 'tis true, but I had a family of servants whom I kept at my business; had a house, shop, and warehouses filled with goods; and, in short, to leave them all as things in such a case must be left (that is to say, without any overseer or person fit to be trusted with them), had been to hazard the loss not only of my trade, but of my goods, and indeed of all I had in the world.

I had an elder brother at the same time in London, and not many years before come over from Portugal: and advising with him, his answer was in three words, the same that was given in another case quite different, viz., 'Master, save thyself.' In a word, he was for my retiring into the country, as he resolved to do himself with his family; telling me what he had, it seems, heard abroad, that the best preparation for the plague was to run away from it. As to my argument of losing my trade, my goods, or debts, he quite confuted me. He told me the same thing which I argued for my staying, viz., that I would trust God with my safety and health, was the strongest repulse to my pretensions of losing my trade and my goods; 'for', says he, 'is it not as reasonable that you should trust God with the chance or risk of losing your trade, as that you should stay in so eminent a point of danger, and trust Him with your life?'

I could not argue that I was in any strait as to a place where to go, having several friends and relations in Northamptonshire, whence our family first came from; and particularly, I had an only sister in Lincolnshire, very willing to receive and entertain me.

My brother, who had already sent his wife and

two children into Bedfordshire, and resolved to
follow them, pressed my going very earnestly; and
I had once resolved to comply with his desires, but
at that time could get no horse; for though it is
true all the people did not go out of the city of
London, yet I may venture to say that in a manner
all the horses did; for there was hardly a horse to
be bought or hired in the whole city for some
weeks. Once I resolved to travel on foot with one
servant, and, as many did, lie at no inn, but carry a
soldier's tent with us, and so lie in the fields, the
weather being very warm, and no danger from
taking cold. I say, as many did, because several did
so at last, especially those who had been in the
armies in the war which had not been many years
past; and I must needs say that, speaking of second
causes, had most of the people that travelled done
so, the plague had not been carried into so many
country towns and houses as it was, to the great
damage, and indeed to the ruin, of abundance of
people.

But then my servant, whom I had intended to
take down with me, deceived me; and being
frighted at the increase of the distemper, and not

knowing when I should go, he took other measures, and left me, so I was put off for that time; and, one way or other, I always found that to appoint to go away was always crossed by some accident or other, so as to disappoint and put it off again; and this brings in a story which otherwise might be thought a needless digression, viz., about these disappointments being from Heaven.

I mention this story also as the best method I can advise any person to take in such a case, especially if he be one that makes conscience of his duty, and would be directed what to do in it, namely, that he should keep his eye upon the particular providences which occur at that time, and look upon them complexly, as they regard one another, and as all together regard the question before him: and then, I think, he may safely take them for intimations from Heaven of what is his unquestioned duty to do in such a case; I mean as to going away from or staying in the place where we dwell, when visited with an infectious distemper.

It came very warmly into my mind one morning, as I was musing on this particular thing, that as nothing attended us without the direction or permission of Divine Power, so these disappointments must have something in them extraordinary; and I ought to consider whether it did not evidently point out, or intimate to me, that it was the will of Heaven I should not go. It immediately followed in my thoughts, that if it really was from God that I should stay, He was able effectually to preserve me in the midst of all the death and danger that would surround me; and that if I attempted to secure myself by fleeing from my habitation, and acted contrary to these intimations, which I believe to be Divine, it was a kind of flying from God, and that He could cause His justice to overtake me when and where He thought fit.

These thoughts quite turned my resolutions again, and when I came to discourse with my brother again I told him that I inclined to stay and take my lot in that station in which God had placed me, and that it seemed to be made more especially my duty, on the account of what I have said.

My brother, though a very religious man himself, laughed at all I had suggested about its being an intimation from Heaven, and told me several stories of such foolhardy people, as he called them, as I was; that I ought indeed to submit to it as a work of Heaven if I had been any way disabled by distempers or diseases, and that then not being able to go, I ought to acquiesce in the direction of Him, who, having been my Maker, had an undisputed right of sovereignty in disposing of me, and that then there had been no difficulty to determine which was the call of His providence and which was not; but that I should take it as an intimation from Heaven that I should not go out of town, only because I could not hire a horse to go, or my fellow was run away that was to attend me, was ridiculous, since at the time I had my health and limbs, and other servants, and might with ease travel a day or two on foot, and having a good certificate of being in perfect health, might either hire a horse or take post on the road, as I thought fit.

Then he proceeded to tell me of the mischievous consequences which attended the presumption of the Turks and Mahometans in Asia and in other places where he had been (for my brother, being a merchant, was a few years before, as I have already observed, returned from abroad, coming last from Lisbon), and how, presuming upon their professed predestinating notions, and of every man's end being predetermined and unalterably beforehand decreed, they would go unconcerned into infected places and converse with infected persons, by which means they died at the rate of ten or fifteen thousand a week, whereas the Europeans or Christian merchants, who kept themselves retired and reserved, generally escaped the contagion.

Upon these arguments my brother changed my resolutions again, and I began to resolve to go, and accordingly made all things ready; for, in short, the infection increased round me, and the bills were risen to almost seven hundred a week, and my brother told me he would venture to stay no longer. I desired him to let me consider of it but till the next day, and I would resolve; and as I had already prepared everything as well as I could as to my business, and whom to entrust my affairs with, I had little to do but to resolve.

I went home that evening greatly oppressed in my mind, irresolute, and not knowing what to do. I had set the evening wholly apart to consider seriously about it, and was all alone; for already people had, as it were by a general consent, taken up the custom of not going out of doors after sunset; the reasons I shall have occasion to say more of by-and-by.

In the retirement of this evening I endeavoured to resolve, first, what was my duty to do, and I stated the arguments with which my brother had pressed me to go into the country, and I set against them the strong impressions which I had on my mind for staying; the visible call I seemed to have from the particular circumstance of my calling, and the care due from me for the preservation of my effects, which were, as I might say, my estate; also the intimations which I thought I had from Heaven, that to me signified a kind of direction to venture; and it occurred to me that if I had what I might call a direction to stay, I ought to suppose it contained a promise of being preserved if I obeyed.

This lay close to me, and my mind seemed more and more encouraged to stay than ever, and supported with a secret satisfaction that I should be kept. Add to this, that, turning over the Bible which lay before me, and while my thoughts were more than ordinarily serious upon the question, I cried out, 'Well, I know not what to do; Lord, direct me!' and the like; and at that juncture I happened to stop turning over the book at the 91st Psalm, and casting my eye on the second verse, I read on to the seventh verse exclusive, and after that included the tenth, as follows: 'I will say of the Lord, He is my refuge and my fortress: my God, in Him will I trust. Surely He shall deliver thee from the snare of the fowler, and from the noisome pestilence. He shall cover thee with His feathers, and under His wings shalt thou trust: His truth shall be thy shield and buckler. Thou shalt not be afraid for the terror by night; nor for the arrow that flieth by day; nor for the pestilence that walketh in darkness; nor for the destruction that wasteth at noonday. A thousand shall fall at thy side, and ten thousand at thy right hand; but it shall not come nigh thee. Only with thine eyes shalt thou behold and see the reward of the wicked. Because thou hast made the Lord, which is my refuge, even the most High, thy habitation; there shall no evil befall thee, neither shall any plague come nigh thy dwelling,' &c.

I scarce need tell the reader that from that moment I resolved that I would stay in the town, and casting myself entirely upon the goodness and protection of the Almighty, would not seek any other shelter whatever; and that, as my times were in His hands, He was as able to keep me in a time of the infection as in a time of health; and if He did not think fit to deliver me, still I was in His hands, and it was meet He should do with me as should seem good to Him.

With this resolution I went to bed; and I was further confirmed in it the next day by the woman being taken ill with whom I had intended to entrust my house and all my affairs. But I had a further obligation laid on me on the same side, for the next day I found myself very much out of order also, so that if I would have gone away, I could not; and I continued ill three or four days, and this entirely determined my stay; so I took my leave of my brother, who went away to Dorking, in Surrey, and afterwards fetched a round farther into Buckinghamshire or Bedfordshire, to a retreat he had found out there for his family.

It was a very ill time to be sick in, for if any one

complained, it was immediately said he had the plague; and though I had indeed no symptoms of that distemper, yet being very ill, both in my head and in my stomach, I was not without apprehension that I really was infected; but in about three days I grew better; the third night I rested well, sweated a little, and was much refreshed. The apprehensions of its being the infection went also quite away with my illness, and I went about my business as usual.

These things, however, put off all my thoughts of going into the country; and my brother also being gone, I had no more debate either with him or with myself on that subject.

It was now mid-July, and the plague, which had chiefly raged at the other end of the town, and, as I said before, in the parishes of St Giles, St Andrew's, Holborn, and towards Westminster, began to now come eastward towards the part where I lived. It was to be observed, indeed, that it did not come straight on towards us; for the city, that is to say, within the walls, was indifferently healthy still; nor was it got then very much over the water into Southwark; for though there died that week

1268 of all distempers, whereof it might be supposed above 900 died of the plague, yet there was but twenty-eight in the whole city, within the walls, and but nineteen in Southwark, Lambeth parish included; whereas in the parishes of St Giles and St Martin-in-the-Fields alone there died 421.

But we perceived the infection kept chiefly in the out-parishes, which being very populous, and fuller also of poor, the distemper found more to prey upon than in the city, as I shall observe afterwards. We perceived, I say, the distemper to draw our way, viz., by the parishes of Clarkenwell, Cripplegate, Shoreditch, and Bishopsgate; which last two parishes joining to Aldgate, Whitechapel, and Stepney, the infection came at length to spread its utmost rage and violence in those parts, even when it abated at the western parishes where it began.

It was very strange to observe that in this particular week, from the 4th to the 11th of July, when, as I have observed, there died near 400 of the plague in the two parishes of St Martin and St Giles-in-the-fields only, there died in the parish of Aldgate but four, in the parish of Whitechapel three, in the parish of Stepney but one.

Likewise in the next week, from the 11th of July to the 18th, when the week's bill was 1761, yet there died no more of the plague, on the whole Southwark side of the water, than sixteen.

But this face of things soon changed, and it began to thicken in Cripplegate parish especially, and in Clarkenwell; so that by the second week in August, Cripplegate parish alone buried 886, and Clarkenwell 155. Of the first, 850 might well be reckoned to die of the plague; and of the last, the bill itself said 145 were of the plague.

During the month of July, and while, as I have observed, our part of the town seemed to be spared in comparison of the west part, I went ordinarily about the streets, as my business required, and particularly went generally once in a day, or in two days, into the city, to my brother's house, which he had given me charge of, and to see if it was safe; and having the key in my pocket, I used to go into the house, and over most of the rooms, to see that all was well; for though it be something wonderful to tell, that any should have hearts so hardened in the midst of such a calamity as to rob and steal, yet certain it is that all sorts of villainies,

and even levities and debaucheries, were then practised in the town as openly as ever — I will not say
quite as frequently, because the numbers of people
were many ways lessened.

But the city itself began now to be visited too,
I mean within the walls; but the number of
people there were indeed extremely lessened by
so great a multitude having been gone into the
country; and even all this month of July they
continued to flee, though not in such multitudes
as formerly. In August, indeed, they fled in such
a manner that I began to think there would be
really none but magistrates and servants left in
the city.

As they fled now out of the city, so I should
observe that the Court removed early, viz., in the
month of June, and went to Oxford, where it
pleased God to preserve them; and the distemper
did not, as I heard of, so much as touch them, for
which I cannot say that I ever saw they showed
any great token of thankfulness, and hardly anything of reformation, though they did not want
being told that their crying vices might without
breach of charity be said to have gone far in

bringing that terrible judgement upon the whole nation.

The face of London was now indeed strangely altered: I mean the whole mass of buildings, city, liberties, suburbs, Westminster, Southwark, and altogether; for as to the particular part called the city, or within the walls, that was not yet much infected. But in the whole the face of things, I say, was much altered; sorrow and sadness sat upon every face; and though some parts were not yet overwhelmed, yet all looked deeply concerned; and, as we saw it apparently coming on, so every one looked on himself and his family as in the utmost danger. Were it possible to represent those times exactly to those that did not see them, and give the reader due ideas of the horror that everywhere presented itself, it must make just impressions upon their minds and fill them with surprise. London might well be said to be all in tears; the mourners did not go about the streets indeed, for nobody put on black or made a formal dress of mourning for their nearest friends; but the voice of mourners was truly heard in the streets. The shrieks of women and children at the windows and doors of their houses, where their dearest relations were perhaps dying, or just dead, were so frequent to be heard as we passed the streets, that it was enough to pierce the stoutest heart in the world to hear them. Tears and lamentations were seen almost in every house, especially in the first part of the visitation; for towards the latter end men's hearts were hardened, and death was so always before their eyes, that they did not so much concern themselves for the loss of their friends, expecting that themselves should be summoned the next hour.

Business led me out sometimes to the other end of the town, even when the sickness was chiefly there; and as the thing was new to me, as well as to everybody else, it was a most surprising thing to see those streets which were usually so thronged now grown desolate, and so few people to be seen in them, that if I had been a stranger and at a loss for my way, I might sometimes have gone the length of a whole street (I mean of the by-streets), and seen nobody to direct me except watchmen set at the doors of such houses as were shut up, of which I shall speak presently.

One day, being at that part of the town on some special business, curiosity led me to observe things more than usually, and indeed I walked a great way where I had no business. I went up Holborn, and there the street was full of people, but they walked in the middle of the great street, neither on one side or other, because, as I suppose, they would not mingle with anybody that came out of houses, or meet with smells and scent from houses that might be infected.

The Inns of Court were all shut up; nor were very many of the lawyers in the Temple, or Lincoln's Inn, or Gray's Inn, to be seen there. Everybody was at peace; there was no occasion for lawyers; besides, it being in the time of the vacation too, they were generally gone into the country. Whole rows of houses in some places were shut close up, the inhabitants all fled, and only a watchman or two left.

When I speak of rows of houses being shut up, I do not mean shut up by the magistrates, but that great numbers of persons followed the Court, by the necessity of their employments and other dependences; and as others retired, really frighted with the distemper, it was a mere desolating of some of the streets. But the fright was not yet near so great in the city, abstractly so called, and particularly because, though they were at first in a most inexpressible consternation, yet as I have observed that the distemper intermitted often at first, so they were, as it were, alarmed and un-alarmed again, and this several times, till it began to be familiar to them; and that even when it appeared violent, yet seeing it did not presently spread into the city, or the east and south parts, the people began to take courage, and to be, as I may say, a little hardened. It is true a vast many people fled, as I have observed, yet they were chiefly from the west end of the town, and from that we call the heart of the city: that is to say, among the wealthiest of the people, and such people as were unencumbered with trades and business. But of the rest, the generality stayed, and seemed to abide the worst; so that in the place we call the Liberties, and in the suburbs, in Southwark, and in the east part, such as Wap-ping, Ratcliff, Stepney, Rotherhithe, and the like, the people generally stayed, except here and there a few wealthy families, who, as above, did not depend upon their business.

It must not be forgot here that the city and suburbs were prodigiously full of people at the time of this visitation, I mean at the time that it began; for though I have lived to see a further increase, and mighty throngs of people settling in London more than ever, yet we had always a notion that the numbers of people which, the wars being over, the armies disbanded, and the royal family and the monarchy being restored, had flocked to London to settle in business, or to depend upon and attend the Court for rewards of services, preferments, and the like, was such that the town was computed to have in it above a hundred thousand people more than ever it held before; nay, some took upon them to say it had twice as many, because all the ruined families of the royal party flocked hither. All the old soldiers set up trades here, and abundance of families settled here. Again, the Court brought with them a great flux of pride, and new fashions. All people were grown gay and luxurious, and the joy of the Restoration had brought a vast many families to London.

I often thought that as Jerusalem was besieged by the Romans when the Jews were assembled together to celebrate the Passover – by which means an incredible number of people were surprised there who would otherwise have been in other countries – so the plague entered London when an incredible increase of people had happened occasionally, by the particular circumstances above-named. As this conflux of the people to a youthful and gay Court made a great trade in the city, especially in everything that belonged to fashion and finery, so it drew by consequence a great number of workmen, manufacturers, and the like, being mostly poor people who depended upon their labour. And I remember in particular that in a representation to my Lord Mayor of the condition of the poor, it was estimated that there were no less than an hundred thousand riband-weavers in and about the city, the chiefest number of whom lived then in the parishes of Shoreditch, Stepney, Whitechapel, and Bishopsgate, that, namely, about Spitalfields; that is to say, as Spitalfields was then, for it was not so large as now by one fifth part.

By this, however, the number of people in the

whole may be judged of; and, indeed, I often wondered that, after the prodigious numbers of people that went away at first, there was yet so great a multitude left as it appeared there was.

But I must go back again to the beginning of this surprising time. While the fears of the people were young, they were increased strangely by several odd accidents which, put altogether, it was really a wonder the whole body of the people did not rise as one man and abandon their dwellings, leaving the place as a space of ground designed by Heaven for an Akeldama, doomed to be destroyed from the face of the earth, and that all that would be found in it would perish with it. I shall name but a few of these things; but sure they were so many, and so many wizards and cunning people propagating them, that I have often wondered there was any (women especially) left behind.

In the first place, a blazing star or comet appeared for several months before the plague, as there did the year after another, a little before the fire. The old women and the phlegmatic hypochondriac part of the other sex, whom I could almost call old women too, remarked (especially afterward, though not till both those judgements were over) that those two comets passed directly over the city, and that so very near the houses that it was plain they imported something peculiar to the city alone; that the comet before the pestilence was of a faint, dull, languid colour, and its motion very heavy, solemn, and slow; but that the comet before the fire was bright and sparkling, or, as others said, flaming, and its motion swift and furious; and that, accordingly, one foretold a heavy judgement, slow but severe, terrible and frightful, as was the plague; but the other foretold a stroke, sudden, swift, and fiery as the conflagration. Nay, so particular some people were, that as they looked upon that comet preceding the fire, they fancied that they not only saw it pass swiftly and fiercely, and could perceive the motion with their eye, but even they heard it; that it made a rushing, mighty noise, fierce and terrible, though at a distance, and but just perceivable.

I saw both these stars, and, I must confess, had so much of the common notion of such things in my head, that I was apt to look upon them as the forerunners and warnings of God's judgements;

and especially when, after the plague had followed the first, I yet saw another of the like kind, I could not but say God had not yet sufficiently scourged the city.

But I could not at the same time carry these things to the height that others did, knowing, too, that natural causes are assigned by the astronomers for such things, and that their motions and even their revolutions are calculated, or pretended to be calculated, so that they cannot be so perfectly called the forerunners or foretellers, much less the procurers, of such events as pestilence, war, fire, and the like.

But let my thoughts and the thoughts of the philosophers be, or have been, what they will, these things had a more than ordinary influence upon the minds of the common people, and they had almost universal melancholy apprehensions of some dreadful calamity and judgement coming upon the city; and this principally from the sight of this comet, and the little alarm that was given in December by two people dying at St Giles's, as above.

The apprehensions of the people were likewise

strangely increased by the error of the times; in which, I think, the people, from what principle I cannot imagine, were more addicted to prophecies and astrological conjurations, dreams, and old wives' tales than ever they were before or since. Whether this unhappy temper was originally raised by the follies of some people who got money by it – that is to say, by printing predictions and prognostications – I know not; but certain it is, books frighted them terribly, such as Lilly's *Almanack*, Gadbury's *Astrological Predictions*, *Poor Robin's Almanack*, and the like; also several pretended religious books, one entitled, *Come out of her, my People, lest you be Partaker of her Plagues*; another called, *Fair Warning*; another, *Britain's Remembrancer*; and many such, all, or most part of which, foretold, directly or covertly, the ruin of the city. Nay, some were so enthusiastically bold as to run about the streets with their oral predictions, pretending they were sent to preach to the city; and one in particular, who, like Jonah to Nineveh, cried in the streets, 'Yet forty days, and London shall be destroyed.' I will not be positive whether he said yet forty days or yet a few days. Another

27

ran about naked, except a pair of drawers about his waist, crying day and night, like a man that Josephus mentions, who cried, 'Woe to Jerusalem!' a little before the destruction of that city. So this poor naked creature cried, 'Oh, the great and the dreadful God!' and said no more, but repeated those words continually, with a voice and countenance full of horror, a swift pace; and nobody could ever find him to stop or rest, or take any sustenance, at least that ever I could hear of. I met this poor creature several times in the streets, and would have spoken to him, but he would not enter into speech with me or any one else, but held on his dismal cries continually.

These things terrified the people to the last degree, and especially when two or three times, as I have mentioned already, they found one or two in the bills dead of the plague at St Giles's.

Next to these public things were the dreams of old women, or, I should say, the interpretation of old women upon other people's dreams; and these put abundance of people even out of their wits. Some heard voices warning them to be gone, for that there would be such a plague in London, so that the living would not be able to bury the dead. Others saw apparitions in the air; and I must be allowed to say of both, I hope without breach of charity, that they heard voices that never spake, and saw sights that never appeared; but the imagination of the people was really turned wayward and possessed. And no wonder, if they who were poring continually at the clouds saw shapes and figures, representations and appearances, which had nothing in them but air and vapour. Here they told us they saw a flaming sword held in a hand coming out of a cloud, with a point hanging directly over the city; there they saw hearses and coffins in the air carrying to be buried; and there again, heaps of dead bodies lying unburied, and the like, just as the imagination of the poor terrified people furnished them with matter to work upon.

> So hypochondriac fancies represent
> Ships, armies, battles in the firmament;
> Till steady eyes the exhalations solve,
> And all to its first matter, cloud, resolve.

I could fill this account with the strange relations

such people gave every day of what they had seen; and every one was so positive of their having seen what they pretended to see, that there was no contradicting them without breach of friendship, or being accounted rude and unmannerly on the one hand, and profane and impenetrable on the other. One time before the plague was begun (otherwise than as I have said in St Giles's), I think it was in March, seeing a crowd of people in the street, I joined with them to satisfy my curiosity, and found them all staring up into the air to see what a woman told them appeared plain to her, which was an angel clothed in white, with a fiery sword in his hand, waving it or brandishing it over his head. She described every part of the figure to the life, showed them the motion and the form, and the poor people came into it so eagerly, and with so much readiness; 'Yes, I see it all plainly,' says one; 'there's the sword as plain as can be.' Another saw the angel. One saw his very face, and cried out what a glorious creature he was! One saw one thing, and one another. I looked as earnestly as the rest, but perhaps not with so much willingness to be imposed upon; and I said, indeed, that I could see nothing but a white cloud, bright on one side by the shining of the sun upon the other part. The woman endeavoured to show it me, but could not make me confess that I saw it, which, indeed, if I had I must have lied. But the woman, turning upon me, looked in my face, and fancied I laughed, in which her imagination deceived her too, for I really did not laugh, but was very seriously reflecting how the poor people were terrified by the force of their own imagination. However, she turned from me, called me profane fellow, and a scoffer; told me that it was a time of God's anger, and dreadful judgements were approaching, and that despisers such as I should wander and perish.

The people about her seemed disgusted as well as she; and I found there was no persuading them that I did not laugh at them, and that I should be rather mobbed by them than be able to undeceive them. So I left them; and this appearance passed for as real as the blazing star itself.

Another encounter I had in the open day also; and this was in going through a narrow passage from Petty France into Bishopsgate Churchyard, by a row of alms-houses. There are two church-yards to Bishopsgate church or parish; one we go over to pass from the place called Petty France into Bishopsgate Street, coming out just by the church door; the other is on the side of the narrow passage where the alms-houses are on the left; and a dwarf-wall with a palisado on it on the right hand, and the city wall on the other side more to the right.

In this narrow passage stands a man looking through between the palisadoes into the burying-place, and as many people as the narrowness of the passage would admit to stop, without hindering the passage of others, and he was talking mighty eagerly to them, and pointing now to one place, then to another, and affirming that he saw a ghost walking upon such a gravestone there. He de-scribed the shape, the posture, and the movement of it so exactly that it was the greatest matter of amazement to him in the world that everybody did not see it as well as he. On a sudden he would cry, 'There it is; now it comes this way.' Then, ' 'Tis turned back'; till at length he persuaded the people into so firm a belief of it, that one fancied he saw it, and another fancied he saw it; and thus he came every day making a strange hubbub, considering it was in so narrow a passage, till Bishopsgate clock struck eleven, and then the ghost would seem to start, and, as if he were called away, disappeared on a sudden.

I looked earnestly every way, and at the very moment that this man directed, but could not see the least appearance of anything; but so positive was this poor man, that he gave the people the vapours in abundance, and sent them away trembling and frighted, till at length few people that knew of it cared to go through that passage, and hardly anybody by night on any account whatever.

This ghost, as the poor man affirmed, made signs to the houses, and to the ground, and to the people, plainly intimating, or else they so understanding it, that abundance of the people should come to be buried in that churchyard, as indeed happened; but that he saw such aspects I must acknowledge I never believed, nor could I see anything of it myself, though I looked most earnestly to see it, if possible.

These things serve to show how far the people were really overcome with delusions; and as they had a notion of the approach of a visitation, all their predictions ran upon a most dreadful plague, which should lay the whole city, and even the kingdom, waste, and should destroy almost all the nation, both man and beast.

To this, as I said before, the astrologers added stories of the conjunctions of planets in a malignant manner and with a mischievous influence, one of which conjunctions was to happen, and did happen, in October, and the other in November; and they filled the people's heads with predictions on these signs of the heavens, intimating that those conjunctions foretold drought, famine, and pestilence. In the two first of them, however, they were entirely mistaken, for we had no droughty season, but in the beginning of the year a hard frost, which lasted from December almost to March, and after that moderate weather, rather warm than hot, with refreshing winds, and, in short, very seasonable weather, and also several very great rains.

Some endeavours were used to suppress the printing of such books as terrified the people, and to frighten the dispersers of them, some of whom were taken up; but nothing was done in it, as I am informed, the Government being unwilling to exasperate the people, who were, as I may say, all out of their wits already.

Neither can I acquit those ministers that in their sermons rather sank than lifted up the hearts of their hearers. Many of them no doubt did it for the strengthening the resolution of the people, and especially for quickening them to repentance, but it certainly answered not their end, at least not in proportion to the injury it did another way; and indeed, as God Himself through the whole Scriptures rather draws to Him by invitations and calls to turn to Him and live, than drives us by terror and amazement, so I must confess I thought the ministers should have done also, imitating our blessed Lord and Master in this, that His whole Gospel is full of declarations from heaven of God's mercy, and His readiness to receive penitents and forgive them, complaining, 'Ye will not come unto Me that ye may have life', and that therefore His Gospel is called the Gospel of Peace and the Gospel of Grace.

But we had some good men, and that of all

persuasions and opinions, whose discourses were full of terror, who spoke nothing but dismal things; and as they brought the people together with a kind of horror, sent them away in tears, prophesying nothing but evil tidings, terrifying the people with the apprehensions of being utterly destroyed, not guiding them, at least not enough, to cry to heaven for mercy.

It was, indeed, a time of very unhappy breaches among us in matters of religion. Innumerable sects and divisions and separate opinions prevailed among the people. The Church of England was restored, indeed, with the restoration of the monarchy, about four years before; but the ministers and preachers of the Presbyterians and Independents, and of all the other sorts of professions, had begun to gather separate societies and erect altar against altar, and all those had their meetings for worship apart, as they have now, but not so many then, the Dissenters being not thoroughly formed into a body as they are since; and those congregations which were thus gathered together were yet but few. And even those that were, the Government did not allow, but endeavoured to suppress them and shut up their meetings.

But the visitation reconciled them again, at least for a time, and many of the best and most valuable ministers and preachers of the Dissenters were suffered to go into the churches where the incumbents were fled away, as many were, not being able to stand it; and the people flocked without distinction to hear them preach, not much inquiring who or what opinion they were of. But after the sickness was over, that spirit of charity abated; and every church being again supplied with their own ministers, or others presented where the minister was dead, things returned to their old channel again.

One mischief always introduces another. These terrors and apprehensions of the people led them into a thousand weak, foolish, and wicked things, which they wanted not a sort of people really wicked to encourage them to: and this was running about to fortune-tellers, cunning-men, and astrologers to know their fortune, or, as it is vulgarly expressed, to have their fortunes told them, their nativities calculated, and the like; and this folly presently made the town swarm with a wicked generation of pretenders to magic, to the black art, as they called it, and I know not what; nay, to a thousand worse dealings with the devil than they were really guilty of. And this trade grew so open and so generally practised that it became common to have signs and inscriptions set up at doors: 'Here lives a fortune-teller', 'Here lives an astrologer', 'Here you may have your nativity calculated', and the like; and Friar Bacon's brazen-head, which was the usual sign of these people's dwellings, was to be seen almost in every street, or else the sign of Mother Shipton, or of Merlin's head, and the like.

With what blind, absurd, and ridiculous stuff these oracles of the devil pleased and satisfied the people I really know not, but certain it is that innumerable attendants crowded about their doors every day. And if but a grave fellow in a velvet jacket, a band, and a black coat, which was the habit those quack-conjurers generally went in, was but seen in the streets the people would follow them in crowds, and ask them questions as they went along.

I need not mention what a horrid delusion this

was, or what it tended to; but there was no remedy for it till the plague itself put an end to it all – and, I suppose, cleared the town of most of those calculators themselves. One mischief was, that if the poor people asked these mock astrologers whether there would be a plague or no, they all agreed in general to answer 'Yes', for that kept up their trade. And had the people not been kept in a fright about that, the wizards would presently have been rendered useless, and their craft had been at an end. But they always talked to them of such-and-such influences of the stars, of the conjunctions of such-and-such planets, which must necessarily bring sickness and distempers, and consequently the plague. And some had the assurance to tell them the plague was begun already, which was too true, though they that said so knew nothing of the matter.

The ministers, to do them justice, and preachers of most sorts that were serious and understanding persons, thundered against these and other wicked practices, and exposed the folly as well as the wickedness of them together, and the most sober and judicious people despised and abhorred them. But it was impossible to make any impression upon the middling people and the working labouring poor. Their fears were predominant over all their passions, and they threw away their money in a most distracted manner upon those whimsies. Maid-servants especially, and men-servants, were the chief of their customers, and their question generally was, after the first demand of 'Will there be a plague?' I say, the next question was, 'Oh, sir! for the Lord's sake, what will become of me? Will my mistress keep me, or will she turn me off? Will she stay here, or will she go into the country? And if she goes into the country, will she take me with her, or leave me here to be starved and undone?' And the like of men-servants.

The truth is, the case of poor servants was very dismal, as I shall have occasion to mention again by-and-by, for it was apparent a prodigious number of them would be turned away, and it was so. And of them abundance perished, and particularly of those that these false prophets had flattered with hopes that they should be continued in their services, and carried with their masters and mistresses into the country; and had not public charity provided for these poor creatures, whose number was exceeding great and in all cases of this nature must be so, they would have been in the worst condition of any people in the city.

These things agitated the minds of the common people for many months, while the first apprehensions were upon them, and while the plague was not, as I may say, yet broken out. But I must also not forget that the more serious part of the inhabitants behaved after another manner. The Government encouraged their devotion, and appointed public prayers and days of fasting and humiliation, to make public confession of sin and implore the mercy of God to avert the dreadful judgement which hung over their heads; and it is not to be expressed with what alacrity the people of all persuasions embraced the occasion; how they flocked to the churches and meetings, and they were all so thronged that there was often no coming near, no, not to the very doors of the largest churches. Also there were daily prayers appointed morning and evening at several churches, and days of private praying at other places; at all which the people attended, I say, with an uncommon devotion. Several private families also, as well of one opinion as of another, kept family fasts, to which they admitted their near relations only. So that, in a word, those people who were really serious and religious applied themselves in a truly Christian manner to the proper work of repentance and humiliation, as a Christian people ought to do.

Again, the public showed that they would bear their share in these things; the very Court, which was then gay and luxurious, put on a face of just concern for the public danger. All the plays and interludes which, after the manner of the French Court, had been set up, and began to increase among us, were forbid to act; the gaming-tables, public dancing-rooms, and music-houses, which multiplied and began to debauch the manners of the people, were shut up and suppressed; and the jack-puddings, merry-andrews, puppet-shows, rope-dancers, and such-like doings, which had bewitched the poor common people, shut up their shops, finding indeed no trade; for the minds of the people were agitated with other things, and a kind of sadness and horror at these things sat upon the countenances even of the common people. Death was before their eyes, and everybody began to think of their graves, not of mirth and diversions.

But even those wholesome reflections – which, rightly managed, would have most happily led the people to fall upon their knees, make confession of their sins, and look up to their merciful Saviour for pardon, imploring His compassion on them in such a time of their distress, by which we might have been as a second Nineveh – had a quite contrary extreme in the common people, who, ignorant and stupid in their reflections as they were brutishly wicked and thoughtless before, were now led by their fright to extremes of folly; and, as I have said before that they ran to conjurers and witches, and all sorts of deceivers, to know what should become of them (who fed their fears, and kept them always alarmed and awake on purpose to delude them and pick their pockets), so they were as mad upon their running after quacks and mountebanks, and every practising old woman, for medicines and remedies; storing themselves with such multitudes of pills, potions, and preservatives, as they were called, that they not only spent their money but even poisoned themselves beforehand for fear of the poison of the infection; and prepared their bodies for the plague, instead of preserving them against it. On the other hand it is incredible and scarce to be imagined, how the posts of houses and corners of streets were plastered over with doctors' bills and papers of ignorant fellows, quacking and tampering in physic, and inviting the people to come to them for remedies, which was generally set off with such flourishes as these, viz.: 'Infallible preventive pills against the plague.' 'Never-failing preservatives against the infection.' 'Sovereign cordials against the corruption of the air.' 'Exact regulations for the conduct of the body in case of an infection.' 'Anti-pestilential pills.' 'Incomparable drink against the plague, never found out before.' 'An universal remedy for the plague.' 'The only true plague water.' 'The royal antidote against all kinds of infection'; – and such a number more that I cannot reckon up; and if I could, would fill a book of themselves to set them down.

Others set up bills to summon people to their lodgings for directions and advice in the case of infection. These had specious titles also, such as these: –

'An eminent High Dutch physician, newly come over from Holland, where he resided during all the time of the great plague last year in Amsterdam, and cured multitudes of people that actually had the plague upon them.'

'An Italian gentlewoman just arrived from Naples, having a choice secret to prevent infection, which she found out by her great experience, and did wonderful cures with it in the late plague there, wherein there died 20,000 in one day.'

'An ancient gentlewoman, having practised with great success in the late plague in this city, anno 1636, gives her advice only to the female sex. To be spoken with,' &c.

'An experienced physician, who has long studied the doctrine of antidotes against all sorts of poison and infection, has, after forty years' practice, arrived to such skill as may, with God's blessing, direct persons how to prevent their being touched by any contagious distemper whatsoever. He directs the poor gratis.'

I take notice of these by way of specimen. I could give you two or three dozen of the like and yet have abundance left behind. 'Tis sufficient from these to apprise any one of the humour of those times, and how a set of thieves and pickpockets not only robbed and cheated the poor people of their money, but poisoned their bodies with odious and fatal preparations; some with mercury, and some with other things as bad, perfectly remote from the thing pretended to, and rather hurtful than serviceable to the body in case an infection followed.

I cannot omit a subtility of one of those quack operators, with which he gulled the poor people to crowd about him, but did nothing for them without money. He had, it seems, added to his bills, which he gave about the streets, this advertisement in capital letters, viz., 'He gives advice to the poor for nothing.'

Abundance of poor people came to him accordingly, to whom he made a great many fine speeches, examined them of the state of their health and of the constitution of their bodies, and told them many good things for them to do, which were of no great moment. But the issue and conclusion of all was, that he had a preparation which if they took such a quantity of every morning, he would pawn his life they should never have the plague;

no, though they lived in the house with people that were infected. This made the people all resolve to have it; but then the price of that was so much, I think 'twas half-a-crown. 'But, sir,' says one poor woman, 'I am a poor almswoman and am kept by the parish, and your bills say you give the poor your help for nothing.' 'Ay, good woman,' says the doctor, 'so I do, as I published there. I give my advice to the poor for nothing, but not my physic.' 'Alas, sir!' says she, 'that is a snare laid for the poor, then, for you give them advice for nothing, that is to say, you advise them gratis, to buy your physic for their money; so does every shop-keeper with his wares.' Here the woman began to give him ill words, and stood at his door all that day, telling her tale to all the people that came, till the doctor finding she turned away his customers, was obliged to call her upstairs again, and give her his box of physic for nothing, which perhaps, too, was good for nothing when she had it.

But to return to the people, whose confusions fitted them to be imposed upon by all sorts of pretenders and by every mountebank. There is no doubt but these quacking sort of fellows raised great gains out of the miserable people, for we daily found the crowds that ran after them were infinitely greater, and their doors were more thronged than those of Dr Brooks, Dr Upton, Dr Hodges, Dr Berwick, or any, though the most famous men of the time. And I was told that some of them got five pounds a day by their physic.

But there was still another madness beyond all this, which may serve to give an idea of the distracted humour of the poor people at that time: and this was their following a worse sort of deceivers than any of these; for these petty thieves only deluded them to pick their pockets and get their money, in which their wickedness, whatever it was, lay chiefly on the side of the deceivers, not upon the deceived. But in this part I am going to mention, it lay chiefly in the people deceived, or equally in both; and this was in wearing charms, philtres, exorcisms, amulets, and I know not what preparations, to fortify the body with them against the plague; as if the plague was not the hand of God, but a kind of possession of an evil spirit, and that it was to be kept off with crossings, signs of the zodiac, papers tied up with so many knots, and certain words or figures written on them, as particularly the word Abracadabra, formed in triangle or pyramid, thus: –

ABRACADABRA
ABRACADABR
ABRACADAB
ABRACADA
ABRACAD
ABRACA
ABRAC
ABRA
ABR
AB
A

Others had the Jesuits'
mark in a cross:
IH
S.

Others nothing but this
mark, thus:

I might spend a great deal of time in my exclamations against the follies, and indeed the wickedness, of those things, in a time of such danger, in a matter of such consequences as this, of a national infection. But my memorandums of these things relate rather to take notice only of the fact, and mention only that it was so. How the poor people found the insufficiency of those things, and how many of them were afterwards carried away in the dead-carts and thrown into the common graves of every parish with these hellish charms and trumpery hanging about their necks, remains to be spoken of as we go along.

All this was the effect of the hurry the people were in, after the first notion of the plague being at hand was among them, and which may be said to be from about Michaelmas 1664, but more particularly after the two men died in St Giles's in the beginning of December; and again, after another alarm in February. For when the plague evidently spread itself, they soon began to see the folly of trusting to those unperforming creatures who had gulled them of their money; and then their fears worked another way, namely, to amazement and stupidity, not knowing what course to take or what to do either to help or relieve themselves. But they ran about from one neighbour's house to another, and even in the streets from one door to another, with repeated cries of, 'Lord, have mercy upon us! What shall we do?'

Indeed, the poor people were to be pitied in one particular thing in which they had little or no relief, and which I desire to mention with a serious awe and reflection, which perhaps every one that reads this may not relish; namely, that whereas death now began not, as we may say, to hover over every one's head only, but to look into their houses and chambers and stare in their faces. Though there might be some stupidity and dulness of the mind (and there was so, a great deal), yet there was a great deal of just alarm sounded into the very inmost soul, if I may so say, of others. Many consciences were awakened; many hard hearts melted into tears; many a penitent confession was made of crimes long concealed. It would wound the soul of any Christian to have heard the dying groans of many a despairing creature, and none durst come near to comfort them. Many a robbery, many a murder, was then confessed aloud, and nobody surviving to record the accounts of it. People might be heard, even into the streets as we passed along, calling upon God for mercy through Jesus Christ, and saying, 'I have been a thief', 'I have been an adulterer', 'I have been a murderer', and the like, and none durst stop to make the least inquiry into such things or to administer comfort to the poor creatures that in the anguish both of soul and body thus cried out. Some of the ministers did visit the sick at first and for a little while, but it was not to be done. It would have been present death to have gone into some houses. The very buriers of the dead, who were the hardenedest creatures in town, were sometimes beaten back and so terrified that they durst not go into houses where the whole families were swept away together, and where the circumstances were more particularly horrible, as some were; but this was, indeed, at the first heat of the distemper.

Time inured them to it all, and they ventured everywhere afterwards without hesitation, as I shall have occasion to mention at large hereafter.

I am supposing now the plague to be begun, as I have said, and that the magistrates began to take the condition of the people into their serious consideration. What they did as to the regulation of the inhabitants and of infected families, I shall speak to by itself; but as to the affair of health, it is proper to mention it here that, having seen the foolish humour of the people in running after quacks and mountebanks, wizards and fortune-tellers, which they did as above, even to madness, the Lord Mayor, a very sober and religious gentleman, appointed physicians and surgeons for relief of the poor – I mean the diseased poor – and in particular ordered the College of Physicians to publish directions for cheap remedies for the poor, in all the circumstances of the distemper. This, indeed, was one of the most charitable and judicious things that could be done at that time, for this drove the people from haunting the doors of every disperser of bills, and from taking down blindly and without consideration poison for physic and death instead of life.

This direction of the physicians was done by a consultation of the whole College; and, as it was particularly calculated for the use of the poor and for cheap medicines, it was made public, so that everybody might see it, and copies were given gratis to all that desired it. But as it is public, and to be seen on all occasions, I need not give the reader of this the trouble of it.

I shall not be supposed to lessen the authority or capacity of the physicians when I say that the violence of the distemper, when it came to its extremity, was like the fire the next year. The fire, which consumed what the plague could not touch, defied all the application of remedies; the fire-engines were broken, the buckets thrown away, and the power of man was baffled and brought to an end. So the plague defied all medicines; the very physicians were seized with it, with their preservatives in their mouths; and men went about prescribing to others and telling them what to do till the tokens were upon them, and they dropped down dead, destroyed by that very enemy they directed others to oppose. This was the case of several physicians, even some of them the most eminent, and of several of the most skilful surgeons. Abundance of quacks too died, who had the folly to trust to their own medicines, which they must needs be conscious to themselves were good for nothing, and who rather ought, like other sorts of thieves, to have run away, sensible of their guilt, from the justice that they could not but expect should punish them as they knew they had deserved.

Not that it is any derogation from the labour or application of the physicians to say they fell in the common calamity; nor is it so intended by me; it rather is to their praise that they ventured their lives so far as even to lose them in the service of mankind. They endeavoured to do good, and to save the lives of others. But we were not to expect that the physicians could stop God's judgements, or prevent a distemper eminently armed from heaven from executing the errand it was sent about.

PENGUIN 60S CLASSICS

APOLLONIUS OF RHODES · *Jason and the Argonauts*

ARISTOPHANES · *Lysistrata*

SAINT AUGUSTINE · *Confessions of a Sinner*

JANE AUSTEN · *The History of England*

HONORÉ DE BALZAC · *The Atheist's Mass*

BASHŌ · *Haiku*

AMBROSE BIERCE · *An Occurrence at Owl Creek Bridge*

JAMES BOSWELL · *Meeting Dr Johnson*

CHARLOTTE BRONTË · *Mina Laury*

CAO XUEQIN · *The Dream of the Red Chamber*

THOMAS CARLYLE · *On Great Men*

BALDESAR CASTIGLIONE · *Etiquette for Renaissance Gentlemen*

CERVANTES · *The Jealous Extremaduran*

KATE CHOPIN · *The Kiss and Other Stories*

JOSEPH CONRAD · *The Secret Sharer*

DANTE · *The First Three Circles of Hell*

CHARLES DARWIN · *The Galapagos Islands*

THOMAS DE QUINCEY · *The Pleasures and Pains of Opium*

DANIEL DEFOE · *A Visitation of the Plague*

BERNAL DÍAZ · *The Betrayal of Montezuma*

FYODOR DOSTOYEVSKY · *The Gentle Spirit*

FREDERICK DOUGLASS · *The Education of Frederick Douglass*

GEORGE ELIOT · *The Lifted Veil*

GUSTAVE FLAUBERT · *A Simple Heart*

BENJAMIN FRANKLIN · *The Means and Manner of Obtaining Virtue*

EDWARD GIBBON · *Reflections on the Fall of Rome*

CHARLOTTE PERKINS GILMAN · *The Yellow Wallpaper*

GOETHE · *Letters from Italy*

HOMER · *The Rage of Achilles*

HOMER · *The Voyages of Odysseus*

PENGUIN 60s CLASSICS

HENRY JAMES · *The Lesson of the Master*
FRANZ KAFKA · *The Judgement* and *In the Penal Colony*
THOMAS À KEMPIS · *Counsels on the Spiritual Life*
HEINRICH VON KLEIST · *The Marquise of O—*
LIVY · *Hannibal's Crossing of the Alps*
NICCOLÒ MACHIAVELLI · *The Art of War*
SIR THOMAS MALORY · *The Death of King Arthur*
GUY DE MAUPASSANT · *Boule de Suif*
FRIEDRICH NIETZSCHE · *Zarathustra's Discourses*
OVID · *Orpheus in the Underworld*
PLATO · *Phaedrus*
EDGAR ALLAN POE · *The Murders in the Rue Morgue*
ARTHUR RIMBAUD · *A Season in Hell*
JEAN-JACQUES ROUSSEAU · *Meditations of a Solitary Walker*
ROBERT LOUIS STEVENSON · *Dr Jekyll and Mr Hyde*
TACITUS · *Nero and the Burning of Rome*
HENRY DAVID THOREAU · *Civil Disobedience* and *Reading*
LEO TOLSTOY · *The Death of Ivan Ilyich*
IVAN TURGENEV · *Three Sketches from a Hunter's Album*
MARK TWAIN · *The Man That Corrupted Hadleyburg*
GIORGIO VASARI · *Lives of Three Renaissance Artists*
EDITH WHARTON · *Souls Belated*
WALT WHITMAN · *Song of Myself*
OSCAR WILDE · *The Portrait of Mr W. H.*

ANONYMOUS WORKS

Beowulf and Grendel
Buddha's Teachings
Gilgamesh and Enkidu

Krishna's Dialogue on the Soul
Tales of Cú Chulaind
Two Viking Romances

READ MORE IN PENGUIN

For complete information about books available from Penguin and how to order them, please write to us at the appropriate address below. Please note that for copyright reasons the selection of books varies from country to country.

IN THE UNITED KINGDOM: Please write to *Dept. EP, Penguin Books Ltd, Bath Road, Harmondsworth, Middlesex UB7 0DA.*

IN THE UNITED STATES: Please write to *Consumer Sales, Penguin USA, P.O. Box 999, Dept. 17109, Bergenfield, New Jersey 07621-0120.* VISA and MasterCard holders call 1-800-253-6476 to order Penguin titles.

IN CANADA: Please write to *Penguin Books Canada Ltd, 10 Alcorn Avenue, Suite 300, Toronto, Ontario M4V 3B2.*

IN AUSTRALIA: Please write to *Penguin Books Australia Ltd, P.O. Box 257, Ringwood, Victoria 3134.*

IN NEW ZEALAND: Please write to *Penguin Books (NZ) Ltd, Private Bag 102902, North Shore Mail Centre, Auckland 10.*

IN INDIA: Please write to *Penguin Books India Pvt Ltd, 706 Eros Apartments, 56 Nehru Place, New Delhi 110 019.*

IN THE NETHERLANDS: Please write to *Penguin Books Netherlands bv, Postbus 3507, NL-1001 AH Amsterdam.*

IN GERMANY: Please write to *Penguin Books Deutschland GmbH, Metzlerstrasse 26, 60594 Frankfurt am Main.*

IN SPAIN: Please write to *Penguin Books S. A., Bravo Murillo 19, 1ᵒ B, 28015 Madrid.*

IN ITALY: Please write to *Penguin Italia s.r.l., Via Felice Casati 20, I-20124 Milano.*

IN FRANCE: Please write to *Penguin France S. A., 17 rue Lejeune, F-31000 Toulouse.*

IN JAPAN: Please write to *Penguin Books Japan, Ishikiribashi Building, 2-5-4, Suido, Bunkyo-ku, Tokyo 112.*

IN GREECE: Please write to *Penguin Hellas Ltd, Dimocritou 3, GR-106 71 Athens.*

IN SOUTH AFRICA: Please write to *Longman Penguin Southern Africa (Pty) Ltd, Private Bag X08, Bertsham 2013.*